The Common Core Readiness Guide to Reading™

TIPS & TRICKS FOR
ANALYZING
STRUCTURE AND
EVALUATING IDEAS

Sandra K. Athans and Robin W. Parente

ROSEN
PUBLISHING®

New York

Published in 2015 by The Rosen Publishing Group, Inc.
29 East 21st Street, New York, NY 10010

Library of Congress Cataloging-in-Publication Data

Athans, Sandra K., 1958–
Tips & tricks for analyzing structure and evaluating ideas/Sandra K. Athans and Robin W. Parente. — First Edition.
    pages cm. — (The Common Core Readiness Guide to Reading)
Includes bibliographical references and index.
ISBN 978-1-4777-7535-6 (library bound) — ISBN 978-1-4777-7537-0 (pbk.) — ISBN 978-1-4777-7538-7 (6-pack)
1. Reading comprehension—Study and teaching (Middle school) 2. Critical thinking in children—Study and teaching (Middle school) 3. Reader-response criticism—Study and teaching (Middle school) 4. Reading—Language experience approach. 5. Reading (Secondary) I. Parente, Robin W. II. Title. III. Title: Tips and tricks for analyzing structure and evaluating ideas.
LB1050.45.A83 2014
428.4071'2—dc23

                                                            2014004695

Manufactured in the United States of America

Contents

Introduction

The Common Core Reading Standards are a set of skills designed to prepare you for entering college or beginning your career. They're grouped into broad College and Career Reading Anchor Standards, and they help you to use reasoning and evidence in ways that will serve you well now and in the future.

The skills build from kindergarten to the twelfth grade, but grades six to eight take the spotlight here. You may have already noticed changes in your classrooms that are based on the standards—deeper-level reading, shorter passages, an emphasis on informational texts, or an overall increase in rigor within your daily activities.

This book will help you understand, practice, and independently apply the skills through easy-to-use "tips and tricks." Gaining mastery of the skills is the goal.

Your teachers may use "close reading" for some of their instruction. During close reading, you read shorter passages more deeply and analytically.

Close reading passages often have rich, complex content. They contain grade-level vocabulary words, sentence

States across the country collaborated with teachers, researchers, and leading experts to design and develop the Common Core standards.

structures, and literary techniques. Reading a short, three-page passage closely could take two to three days or more. The benefit is that you get a deeper, more valuable understanding of what you've read. Close reading is a critical part of the new Common Core Reading Standards and is used throughout this book.

Other well-known reading comprehension skills remain valuable. Visualizing, asking questions, synthesizing, and other traditional strategies work well together with the Common Core skills covered here.

This book focuses on Anchor Standard 5: analyzing the structure of texts to determine how specific sentences, paragraphs, and larger portions of the text relate to each other and the whole. In chapter 1, we'll break these skills apart and look at them closely. Also, the tips and tricks that can help you gain mastery of this standard are introduced. Some feature visual icons that will be used throughout this book.

In the passages that follow, you tag along with expert readers as they think aloud while close reading from different passages of literature (fiction) and informational text (nonfiction). Visual icons that represent the tips and tricks appear in the margins and prompt the expert reader. Ways in which the expert reader applies them appear in expert-reader margin notes. You'll also review multiple-choice and written response questions completed by the expert readers. Explanations that support their reasoning are provided.

After you gain an understanding of how the skill is applied, then it's your turn to try with guided practice. You'll apply the skill independently and perform a self-evaluation by checking your responses against answers provided. Based on your responses, you can determine if another pass through the expert reader's examples might be helpful— or if you've mastered the skill.

CHAPTER 1

A QUICK AND EASY OVERVIEW: THE SKILLS AND THE TIPS & TRICKS

Let's examine the skills needed for analyzing structure and evaluating ideas closely so that we understand them. We know that the word "analyze" is a verb, so it's something we actively do. When you analyze while reading, you carefully examine, inspect, and consider the text to fully understand it. As you analyze text, you must rely on its content—not on knowledge you gained elsewhere. You may have to break down text into smaller, more manageable units to understand it more fully.

You may also need to make inferences about ideas or events not explicitly stated. An inference is a conclusion you make by interpreting clues provided in the passage—it's as if you're reading between the lines. Your inferences must be reasonably based on something concrete in the text.

In this standard, you will be looking at the structure of texts, specifically how smaller components fit together and contribute to the development of the whole text. This process will involve taking a close look at individual components of a work, including sentences, paragraphs, chapters, sections, scenes, stanzas, or other segments to

One of the key requirements of the Common Core Reading Standards is that all students must be able to comprehend texts of steadily increasing complexity as they progress through school. Often, students are asked to demonstrate their reading abilities through written responses to carefully designed questions.

understand them more fully. Also, analyzing the way in which they help contribute to the development or refinement of ideas, key concepts, theme, plot, and/or setting of a work is another avenue we will consider while building our skills with this standard.

These skills are useful as you read literature and informational text, as well as reading history/social studies, science, and technical subjects. They're also useful for many of your daily real-life activities. As you will

Quick Check Self-Evaluation for Analyzing Structure and Evaluating Ideas

Determining how well you've mastered the tips and tricks for analyzing structure and ideas is important. One way to do this is by gauging your success with the following tasks:

√ I can summarize the passage.

√ My summary is cohesive and makes sense based on evidence.

√ I can identify a theme or key idea and express how the author develops and supports it through specific text-based evidence.

see, there are mild nuances in the manner in which you apply these skills to the different genres. Yet, with practice, these adjustments become automatic.

As you progress in grade levels, you're expected to analyze text structures more deeply as well as more broadly in terms of the ways in which they interact together. Likewise, making comparisons between two or more texts and analyzing their differing structures is another direction in which to extend and develop this skill.

Tips and Tricks

There are several easy-to-use tips and tricks that can help you analyze the structures and ideas within reading passages. Some are useful as you begin to read, while others guide you throughout your reading. Here's a quick overview of them. The icons featured below are used in subsequent chapters to show you how the tips and tricks are used in action with literature and informational texts.

● **Launching "Jump-Start" Clues:** Before you dive into reading a piece of text, skim it. Notice and take a visual inventory of everything you see. The title, subheadings, boldface print, and other features like photographs or charts will give you valuable clues about the content and genre. Authors select and use text features purposefully. It's often helpful to ask yourself, "What could the title mean or what purpose do the special features serve?"

● **Using Genre to Guide Understanding:** You already know a lot about the different genres and common elements that are unique to each. For example, in works of fiction, characters and a setting are introduced, a problem is identified, and events lead to a solution or improvement. With informational text, authors organize ideas in cause and effect or other structures that help readers grasp and remember important information. Working with this knowledge to guide and validate your understanding and analysis is helpful. You might ask yourself, "Does the story unfold in a way that makes sense or does the information seem valid and cohesive?"

● **Be Attentive to the Author:** It's important to detect what the author is saying. In literature, authors often present a life lesson or worthwhile idea through their carefully crafted writing. Ask yourself, "What big idea is the author sharing with me and how has he or she chosen to do this?" Nonfiction and informational text is filtered through the author's perspective. Knowing this is important as you determine the critical ideas of a passage. It's helpful to ask yourself, "What point or issue has the author stressed and how was this accomplished?" It's also important to recognize that in both cases, the author may not be explicit. As a result, you may have to infer the meaning from clues.

● **Tune in to Your Inside Voice:** Your mind is actively making sense as you read. Listening to your thoughts or your mind's dialogue helps you grasp meaning. Connecting new ideas to known ideas is the way your mind builds cohesive meaning. Monitoring your thoughts, including your questions, is critical. Do characters' motives, events in the story, and/or ideas seem unusual or out of place? How do charts, tables, or other special features included within a passage build your understanding? Are your reactions likely what the author intended? Authors often build reader engagement by posing questions. However, it's also important for you to distinguish when you're confused and need to implement fix-up strategies like rereading.

Helping students develop critical thinking skills is fundamental. The Common Core Standards emphasize this as a measure to help prepare students for college and career readiness.

● **Avoid Common Pitfalls:** Sometimes we can become distracted by something in the text, which could steer us away from an author's intended meaning. Staying engaged and focused while ensuring that your ideas are supported by text-based evidence is critical. It's sometimes helpful to validate your interpretation by considering your answer to the following statement: "I know this because…" Your answer to this question must be found within the passage.

As you practice and gain skill with these tips and tricks, you'll find that they work together and often become indistinguishable. This is a sign that they've become authentic and automatic and kick in when and where they're needed.

● **Using Craft and Text Structure:** Looking closely at how authors of literature and informational text carefully construct, craft, and develop their ideas can also help us gain a comprehensive understanding of a work. Specifically determining how components such as sentences and paragraphs or lines and stanzas help develop theme, plot, or setting is a way for us to do this. Looking critically at smaller units of composition and explaining how they fit into the larger passage is like analyzing the many building materials used to construct a home—cement foundation, wooden framework, and sheetrock walls. Each contributes to the complete home. Uncovering how smaller ideas are developed in the larger passage help us uncover how we construct meaning from a passage.

CHAPTER 2

ANALYZING STRUCTURE AND EVALUATING IDEAS IN LITERATURE: EXPERT READER MODEL

Let's see how to apply the tips and tricks to literature. Remember that literature can be adventure stories, historical fiction, mysteries, myths, science fiction, realistic fiction, allegories, parodies, plays, poetry, and more.

Some types of literature, such as narrative fiction, often feature similar elements, including characters, problems or conflicts, a setting and plot, events and episodes, and the resolution of a problem. Authors weave these elements together carefully, mindful that they interact in meaningful and engaging ways. Looking closely at these elements and their interaction gives us a richer understanding of the story. When we explore these elements deeply, it is also more likely that our understanding is in keeping with the author's intention.

Poetry is another specialized form of literature that includes unique characteristics. For example, poetry often includes figurative language, imagery, personification, rhythm, rhyme, repetition, alliteration, and other techniques. Poets use these elements to create sensory imagery

and to stir reader emotion. Even the layout of poetry looks different than the prose of a narrative story. There are also organizational types, or forms, of poetry such as free verse, lyrical poetry, sonnets, and more. Poets select the form to fit an intended meaning and purpose.

Your ability to analyze elements that are unique to these and other forms of literature relies on your grade-level knowledge of literature basics.

Plan of Action

There are two passages in this chapter. Although they do not contain similar subjects or themes, the process of analyzing their structures is similar. You'll be reading the passages and following an expert reader think through a sampling of the tips and tricks in the margin notes. As you tag along with the expert reader, ways in which you analyze the structure will become clear. You'll also observe the expert reader perform a self-evaluation by sharing a summary and the thinking behind it. Then, you'll tag along as the expert reader tackles some multiple-choice questions and a written response question. All activities demonstrate how to analyze structure and evaluate ideas in literature.

After this, it's your turn to practice. In chapter 3, you'll be reading passages where guided practice prompts cue your use of the tips and tricks for literature. You can check your thinking against provided possible responses.

Robert Frost (1874–1963) was an American poet whose work often reflects rural themes. Here, he is pictured on his farm in Vermont. "The Pasture," one of Frost's early poems, is analyzed on the following pages.

📖 EXPERT READER:

I notice this text doesn't look like prose. There's a lot of space and the words seem organized in lines and stanzas. I'm pretty sure this is a poem. It has something to do with a pasture.

G I'm certain this is a poem. I recognize the name Robert Frost, and I know he is a poet. I'll have to read carefully and watch for poetic techniques.

I can't assume this is the poet's point of view, even though it's written in first person. The speaker is going to clean something in the pasture.

The word "spring" is a homophone and has many meanings. I must monitor how this is used.

I'm certain "spring" is a water source in the pasture. The speaker is going to remove the leaves from the spring and then may wait to be sure it flows again. It's possible the speaker is a farmer.

The last line in this first stanza seems significant. It lingers as the last thought, and we realize the speaker isn't alone and invites someone along, even though he has just revealed he will not be gone long.

I think the "you" could be a child. It could explain why the speaker "assures" the child he won't be gone long, and then invites the child along. I'll see if this squares with the evidence in the second stanza.

The speaker is on another pasture errand, this time tending to a young calf.

Fetch means "to retrieve," so the speaker is retrieving the calf even though it's with its mother.

The poet has repeated this line and it is the final line in the stanza. Both support its importance. Inviting the guest along is a detail we mustn't miss.

"The Pasture" 🏃

By Robert Frost G

I'm going out to clean the pasture spring; 🔊 👤💭
I'll only stop to rake the leaves away
(And wait to watch the water clear, I may): 👤💭
I sha'n't be gone long.—You come too. 📝 🔊

I'm going out to fetch the little calf
That's standing by the mother. It's so young. 📝 👤💭
It totters when she licks it with her tongue.
I sha'n't be gone long.—You come too. 🔊

Quick Check Self-Evaluation for Analyzing Structure and Evaluating Ideas

Let's take a break here to let the expert reader summarize and analyze this poem:

In this poem, the speaker must routinely leave on brief errands to the pasture to oversee a variety of tasks that are among his responsibilities. In the first stanza the speaker clears leaves from a spring, and in the second stanza he fetches a young calf. The speaker assures someone, likely a child, that he "sha'n't be gone long" yet then invites the "child" to accompany him. One theme in the poem could be about reassurance; all things in the pasture will be cared for and the "child" will, too.

Expert Reader: I'm satisfied with this summary. I thought carefully about the lines and the stanzas, reread them several times to check my understanding against text evidence, and I'm able to support my ideas. I'm ready to challenge my thinking by answering multiple-choice and written response questions.

Mini Assessment

1. The poet expresses ideas in the poem using the structure of a quatrain, two four-line stanzas that include an ABBC rhyming scheme. How does this idea contribute to the poem's meaning?

a) The structure helps to create a gentle playfulness that supports the idea that the poem could be intended to be read aloud to a child.

b) The structure shows how farmers can also use poetic technique to help readers visualize farm events.

c) The structure supports the belief that all poems should include rhyme, especially if they are to appeal to a young audience.

d) The brief, four-line structure is appealing to young audiences.

2. Which line in the poem signals a major change in the focus of the quatrain?

a) "I'm going out to fetch the little calf."

b) "I'll only stop to rake the leaves away."

c) "I sha'n't be gone long.—You come too."

d) (And wait to watch the water clear, I may.)

Check your answers. Were you correct?

1. a) is the correct answer. The question asks me to identify the poet's likely intentions about the poem's structure. Responses b) and c) do not make sense, while response a) addresses both the line and the rhyming patterns and is therefore a better answer than d).

2. c) is the correct answer. In this line, the speaker pauses from describing the chores he will tackle and directly addresses the listener to invite him along.

Expert Reader: I'm satisfied with my responses. In all cases, I returned to the text to check against evidence. Sometimes the evidence was right there, other times I had to dig a little deeper and use clues and inferences. In either case, my answers square with the evidence. Now I'm ready to try the second passage.

Edgar Allan Poe (1809–1849) was an influential American author, poet, editor, and literary critic. His work continues to appear in popular culture today. "The Bells," analyzed on the following pages, was one of the final poems he wrote.

"The Bells"
(Stanzas I and III)
By Edgar Allan Poe

I

Hear the sledges with the bells—
Silver bells!
What a world of merriment their melody foretells!
How they tinkle, tinkle, tinkle,
In the icy air of night! G
While the stars that oversprinkle
All the heavens, seem to twinkle
With a crystalline delight;
Keeping time, time, time,
In a sort of Runic rhyme,
To the tintinnabulation that so musically wells
From the bells, bells, bells, bells,
Bells, bells, bells—
From the jingling and the tinkling of the bells.

III

Hear the loud alarum bells—
Brazen bells!
What tale of terror, now, their turbulency tells!
In the startled ear of night
How they scream out their affright!
Too much horrified to speak,
They can only shriek, shriek,
Out of tune, G
In a clamorous appealing to the mercy of the fire,
In a mad expostulation with the deaf and frantic fire,

**EXPERT
READER:**

I realize these bells describe sounds from a fire. The lines are shorter and faster. They mimic the kind of frenzy of fire and the helplessness of victims.

**EXPERT
READER:**

The "sounds" throughout this stanza are louder and linger longer than in the first. Also, the poet builds tension line by line, using structure and technique to grip our emotion.

Leaping higher, higher, higher,
With a desperate desire,
And a resolute endeavor
Now—now to sit or never,
By the side of the pale-faced moon.
Oh, the bells, bells, bells!
What a tale their terror tells
Of Despair!
How they clang, and clash, and roar!
What a horror they outpour
On the bosom of the palpitating air!
Yet the ear, it fully knows,
By the twanging,
And the clanging,
How the danger ebbs and flows;
Yet, the ear distinctly tells,
In the jangling,
And the wrangling,
How the danger sinks and swells,
By the sinking or the swelling in the anger of the bells—
Of the bells—
Of the bells, bells, bells, bells,
Bells, bells, bells—
In the clamour and the clangour of the bells!

Quick Check Self-Evaluation for Analyzing Structure and Evaluating Ideas

Let's take a break here to let the expert reader summarize and analyze this poem:

In this poem, we experience sounds, sights, and images of bells that stir our emotions in diverse ways. In the first stanza, the poet sparks our festive spirits by helping us see, hear, and experience tinkling sleigh bells on a clear winter evening. The tone is joyful and merry. In the next stanza, we are terrorized by the shriek of sirens and fire alarms. They swell and race through the air. We are horrified as the fire climbs higher. One theme in the poem is that life events are often unpredictable. Sometimes, good things can swiftly turn bad.

Expert Reader: I'm satisfied with this summary. I thought carefully about the lines and the stanzas, reread them several times to check my understanding against text evidence, and I'm able to support my ideas. I'm ready to challenge my thinking by answering multiple-choice and written response questions.

Mini Assessment

1. How does the use of repetition in both stanzas contribute to the poem as a whole?

a) It emphasizes the poet's well-known and distinctive style.

b) It helps add "sound" to the poem and echoes the repetitive sound made by bells.

c) It helps readers remember the title of the poem.

d) It is a technique many readers enjoy in poetry.

As you practice and gain skill with these tips and tricks, they often work together and become indistinguishable. This often means they are becoming authentic and automatic.

2. Throughout the poem, the line lengths vary greatly and help establish a poetic rhythm. How does this contribute to the poem's meaning?

    a) The rhythm creates a soothing calmness from stanza I to stanza III.

    b) The rhythm is steady and even from stanza I to stanza III.

    c) The rhythm adjusts to the shorter stanza I and the longer stanza III.

    d) The rhythm speeds up and builds tension from stanza I to stanza III.

Check your answers. Were you correct?

1. b) is the correct answer. This is the best answer to the question, as it emphasizes the link between the effects of sound as a technique and the content of the poem.

d) is the correct answer. The fast-moving pace of the poem creates an almost frenzied tension as the reader moves from one stanza to the other.

Expert Reader: I'm satisfied with my responses. I returned to the text to check against evidence. Sometimes it was right there. Other times I had to think carefully and review specific lines in each stanza. Now I feel I'm ready to try a written response question.

Question: The moods of "The Pasture" by Robert Frost and "The Bells" by Edgar Allan Poe are very different. Describe the mood of each and explain how the poem's structure contributes to the mood.

Possible Response: In "The Pasture," the mood of the poem is calm and gentle. The speaker makes a point to invite a guest (possibly a child) to "come too" and accompany him on chores. He does this even after assuring the child that he "sha'n't be gone long." Lines that express tenderness toward the child are repeated, and there is a simple rhyming scheme that mimics the honesty of the poem. On the other hand, the mood of "The Bells" is turbulent. In stanza I, we ease into the festive sound of sleigh bells through the poet's use of repetition, alliteration, and other poetic techniques. Yet, the mood of stanza III changes immediately. The poet uses the same technique although the sounds and images are harsh and disturbing. Stanza III is longer and contains lines that vary greatly in length, which makes us feel uneasy and anxious. Each poet has used structure in a way that supports the meaning of the poem.

Conclusion

How well have you grasped the expert reader's use of the tips and tricks to analyze structure and evaluate ideas? Decide if you're ready to move on to the guided practice in the next chapter or if you would like to take another pass through the expert reader's model.

CHAPTER 3

ANALYZING STRUCTURE AND EVALUATING IDEAS IN LITERATURE: GUIDED PRACTICE

Now it is time for you to apply the tips and tricks during your close reading of two poetry passages. The practice prompt icons will guide you. Check whether your responses to the prompts match possible responses provided.

Birds build nests to protect eggs and the nestlings from predators. Yet some nests are abandoned in response to a disturbance—as explored in "The Exposed Nest" by Robert Frost.

"The Exposed Nest"
By Robert Frost 🏃 G

You were forever finding some new play.
So when I saw you down on hands and knees
In the meadow, busy with the new-cut hay,
Trying, I thought, to set it up on end,
I went to show you how to make it stay,
If that was your idea, against the breeze,
And, if you asked me, even help pretend
To make it root again and grow afresh.🔊
But 'twas no make-believe with you to-day,📑
Nor was the grass itself your real concern,
Though I found your hand full of wilted fern,
Steel-bright June-grass, and blackening heads of clover.
'Twas a nest full of young birds on the ground
The cutter-bar had just gone champing over
(Miraculously without tasting flesh)
And left defenseless to the heat and light.
You wanted to restore them to their right 👥💭
Of something interposed between their sight
And too much world at once—could means be found.
The way the nest-full every time we stirred
Stood up to us as to a mother-bird
Whose coming home has been too long deferred,
Made me ask would the mother-bird return
And care for them in such a change of scene
And might our meddling make her more afraid.
That was a thing we could not wait to learn.
We saw the risk we took in doing good,

GUIDED PRACTICE PROMPT:

🏃 What jump-start clues do you notice? (Possible response: "The Exposed Nest" is a poem by Robert Frost. It is about a nest. The word "exposed" means out in the open. I'll see how my view of the title squares with the content.)

G How can knowledge of genre help guide your understanding? (Possible response: This poem has one stanza, which could mean it contains one central idea or event.)

🔊 Are you being attentive to the author? The "you" in the poem is a child. The speaker, who is older, is recalling a time when he planned to join in the child's pretend play in a meadow. The poem is a recollection.

📑 How can I use text structure to build and check understanding? (Possible response: The author's use of the word "but" at the beginning of this line has my attention. It signals a problem.)

💭 What are you thinking? (Possible response: The child's desire to restore the defenseless nest seems critical, especially after the baby birds unexplainably escaped the cutting machine. This could be a metaphor.)

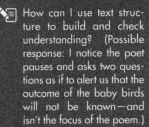

💻 GUIDED PRACTICE PROMPT:

📝 How can I use text structure to build and check understanding? (Possible response: The author's use of the word "but" at the beginning of this line has my attention. It echoes the earlier line and introduces another problem—their disregard of the risks of altering the nest.)

📝 How can I use text structure to build and check understanding? (Possible response: I notice the poet pauses and asks two questions as if to alert us that the outcome of the baby birds will not be known—and isn't the focus of the poem.)

But dared not spare to do the best we could 📝
Though harm should come of it; so built the screen
You had begun, and gave them back their shade.
All this to prove we cared. Why is there then
No more to tell? We turned to other things.
I haven't any memory—have you?—
Of ever coming to the place again
To see if the birds lived the first night through,
And so at last to learn to use their wings. 📝

Quick Check Self-Evaluation for Analyzing Structure and Evaluating Ideas

Now you'll want to summarize the poem and think about the meaning the poet intended. Be sure to review the criteria on page 9. How are you interpreting the poem? How do your ideas square with evidence? Go ahead and try it. Talk it through or get a piece of paper and write it down. Once you're satisfied and have checked your response, challenge your thinking and answer the multiple-choice questions that follow.

Expert Reader's Summary: In this poem, a speaker intends to join in the play of a young person who is crouched among the hay in a meadow. The speaker learns that the child has found a nest of baby birds on the ground. Together the two restore the nest to a safe, shaded area, knowing that their actions might risk the mother's return. Still, they did the best they could, and they never returned to learn of the outcome.

One theme in the poem is about compassion: the inborn compassion we have for protecting and preserving fragile things.

Mini Assessment

1. Which line signals a major change in the tone of the poem?

    a) "I went to show you how to make it stay."

    b) "You wanted to restore them to their right."

    c) "You were forever finding some new play."

    d) "But 'twas no make-believe with you to-day."

2. Reread the following lines from the poem:

"All this to prove we cared. Why is there then
No more to tell? We turned to other things.
I haven't any memory—have you?—"

How do these ideas contribute to the meaning of the poem?

    a) They stress the process of "saving" the nest over the outcome.

    b) They reinforce that the speaker may have been older and forgetful.

    c) They wanted to return to the meadow where they could play.

    d) The poet wants to verify that he has retold the story correctly.

Check your answers. Were you correct?

1. d) is the best answer. The speaker believed the child was playing and intended to join in, yet he quickly learns that the child is instead concerned about restoring the nest.

2. a) is the best answer. Rethinking the event as if it were a memory, the speaker (and child) are unable to recall the outcome. The lasting memory is of saving the nest.

The Spanish conquistadors of the 1500s searched in vain for the legendary city of gold known as Eldorado. Edgar Allan Poe's poem "Eldorado" is analyzed on the opposite page.

Eldorado

By Edgar Allan Poe 🏃

(Note to the reader: The name Eldorado means "the golden one" in Spanish. In the 1500s, the Spanish conquistadors gave this name to a legendary city of gold believed to be somewhere in South America. Explorers never located the city. The poem "Eldorado" was published in a Boston newspaper in 1849, around the time of the California Gold Rush.) G

Gaily bedight,
A gallant knight,
In sunshine and in shadow,
Had journeyed long,
Singing a song,
In search of Eldorado. 💭

But he grew old— G
This knight so bold—
And o'er his heart a shadow
Fell as he found
No spot of ground
That looked like Eldorado. 💭

And, as his strength
Failed him at length,
He met a pilgrim shadow—
"Shadow," said he,
"Where can it be—
This land of Eldorado?" 🔊

GUIDED PRACTICE PROMPT:

🏃 What jump-start clues do you notice? (Possible response: This is a poem by Edgar Allan Poe. It comprises four stanzas and there is a note to the reader, which most likely includes information that will help me interpret the poem.)

G How can I use text structure to build and check understanding? (Possible response: This reader's note is a clue about the title. The history will probably be important to my interpretation of the poem.)

💭 What are you thinking? (Possible response: In this stanza a knight who is seeking Eldorado seems hopeful. He is gallant, at times it's sunny, and the knight even sings. This seems to be a poem about his quest.)

G How can I use text structure to build and check understanding? (Possible response: As this new stanza begins, a problem begins to form. Also, the poet leads the new stanza with "but," a word that signals a disturbance.)

💭 What are you thinking? (Possible response: The knight is growing old, yet is unable to locate Eldorado. As a result he's becoming disheartened.)

🔊 (Possible response: The poet has the very weakened knight meet a "pilgrim shadow" who could symbolize death. This stanza continues to develop the idea that this is a tragic quest for the knight.)

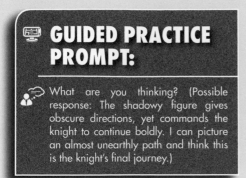

GUIDED PRACTICE PROMPT:

What are you thinking? (Possible response: The shadowy figure gives obscure directions, yet commands the knight to continue boldly. I can picture an almost unearthly path and think this is the knight's final journey.)

"Over the mountains
Of the Moon,
Down the Valley of the Shadow,
Ride, boldly ride,"
The shade replied—
"If you seek for Eldorado!"

Quick Check Self-Evaluation for Analyzing Structure and Evaluating Ideas

Can you summarize this poem in a manner that shows your interpretation squares with the meaning the poet intended? You might want to talk it through or get a piece of paper and write it down. Once you're satisfied and have checked your response, challenge your thinking and answer the multiple-choice questions that follow.

Expert Reader's Summary: In this poem, a knight is on a quest in search of Eldorado. At first, the knight seems hopeful; he joyfully sings despite the long journey. Yet in the second stanza, this changes. The knight has grown old and is still unable to locate Eldorado. As a result, "a shadow" falls over his heart. In the third stanza, the knight has no strength left yet asks directions from a "pilgrim shadow." The shadow directs the knight along a shadowy path. One theme in the poem is about the tragedy of striving for the impossible: Eldorado is a nonexistent legendary place and spending a lifetime trying to search for it could symbolize the wasted search for an unattainable goal.

Mini Assessment

1. What purpose does the reader's note best serve?

    a) It places the poem in a historical context that helps readers identify it as an extended metaphor or allegory.

    b) It foreshadows the tragedy that many of the California gold miners faced when they were unable to find gold.

    c) It helps alert readers that the tone of the poem will likely change with each stanza.

    d) It reflects the importance of spotlighting cultural diversity in literature.

2. How does the end rhyme pattern in lines 3 and 6 in each stanza contribute to the meaning of the poem?

    a) It mimics the joyfulness of the knight's singing in the first stanza, which helps to connect the four stanzas.

    b) It reflects the poet's skill using off-rhythm rhyme.

    c) Eldorado is likened to a shadow, supporting the idea that it doesn't exist.

    d) It helps readers create a visual image of Eldorado in the moonlight, as it is hidden among the mountain shadows.

Check your answers. Were you correct?

1. a) is the best answer. Understanding historical details about the legendary Eldorado gives readers insights that could help them construct meaning from the poem.

2. c) is the best answer. The off rhyme calls attention to the vague and ambiguous similarities between Eldorado and shadows.

How did you do? Is your understanding and analysis of the poem solid? Did you return to the passage and find evidence to support your responses? Are you comfortable discussing or writing an answer to a written response question? Either talk through your answer or write it down on a separate piece of paper. Then, check your answer against the response provided. Remember that it's OK if your answer is different from the one provided. What matters is that you can support your views with text evidence.

Question: In "The Exposed Nest" by Robert Frost and "Eldorado" by Edgar Allan Poe, someone is trying to achieve something, yet the outcomes are very different. For each poem, identify the pursuit and then describe how the structure of the poem supports the outcome. Use evidence to support your answer.

Possible Response: In "The Exposed Nest," a child and adult must pause from their imaginary play to rescue a fallen nest that is filled with baby birds. In the end, we never learn what becomes of the birds as the pair "turned to other things." The narrator in this poem is the adult, and he tells the story as a recollection. This structure allows us to

Your interpretation of a reading passage should reflect your careful thinking. Even if your views differ from others, what matters is that you're able to support them with text evidence.

grasp the speaker's devotion to the child. He speaks tenderly of wanting to play with the child and then joins in the rescue, doing the "best we could" to restore the nest to safety. Sharing the experience of trying to save the nest with a child was valued more than the outcome of the mission. In "Eldorado," a gallant knight is on a lengthy quest in search of Eldorado. In the end, he never finds Eldorado despite having spent his entire life trying. This poem is told from a third-person point of view. This structure keeps us at a distance from the knight and makes us unsure of his motives. Also, the poem is organized in four stanzas, which emphasizes the passing of time. Last, the note to the reader informs us that others have chased dreams that never came true. All evidence suggests that the outcome of the knight's quest was tragic. He, like many others before him, spent his life chasing shadows.

Conclusion

How well have you grasped the tips and tricks for analyzing structure and evaluating ideas in literature? Based on your performance and self-evaluation, decide if you're ready to move on to the next chapter or if you would like to take another pass through this guided practice.

CHAPTER 4

ANALYZING STRUCTURE AND EVALUATING IDEAS IN INFORMATIONAL TEXT: EXPERT READER MODEL

Now, let's see how to apply the tips and tricks to informational text. Informational text is a type of nonfiction, or factual, text that is written to inform the reader, explain something, or convey information about the natural and social worlds. Informational text can include newspaper articles, magazine articles, essays, speeches, opinion pieces, editorials, and historical, scientific, technical, or economic accounts.

Authors of informational text have a point to make about a topic. They frequently want to change your thinking in some way or add to your understanding. These authors purposefully organize their ideas by using descriptive, compare/contrast, cause/effect, chronological/sequence, or problem/solution text structures. Awareness of these structures helps a reader evaluate ideas and improves comprehension of the text.

Plan of Action

This section contains an excerpt from *Science Made Simple: Electric and Magnetic Phenomena*. As you did previously, you'll be reading the excerpt while following an expert reader think through the tips and tricks—this time as they are applied to informational text. You may want to refresh your memory by reviewing the tips and tricks before beginning.

Again, you'll observe the expert reader perform a self-evaluation through the sharing of a summary and the thinking behind it. Finally, you'll tag along while the expert reader works through some multiple-choice questions and a constructed response question to get the full impact of how to analyze text structure and evaluate ideas in informational text.

Then, in the chapter that follows, it will be your turn to practice. You'll start by reading a passage where guided practice prompts and icons cue your use of the tips and tricks. You can check your thinking against possible provided responses.

EXPERT READER:

I notice this text is arranged into sections, with headings and subheadings. I also notice the content area into which this text will most likely fall (scientific). I wonder what the title could mean. What is phenomena?

G I'm certain this is informational text. As I read, I'll notice how ideas build on one another and pay attention to how the text is organized into sections. I know authors do this to help readers grasp important ideas.

An Excerpt from: *Science Made Simple: Electric and Magnetic Phenomena*
by Dean Galiano

Introduction G

Throughout history, people have witnessed electrical and magnetic phenomena. For many centuries, however, these phenomena were not understood. Ancient people

In northern latitudes, the auroras may be seen high overhead, but when seen from farther away, they illuminate the horizon with a greenish or faint red glow.

observed the glowing auroras near the North and South poles of Earth, but they had no idea what caused these mysterious lights. It is now known that the auroras are caused by electrically charged particles being drawn into Earth's atmosphere, but ancient people had no scientific way to explain the lights. They could only imagine that supernatural forces, such as gods or spirits of dead relatives, produced the lights. 〽

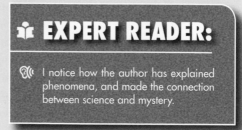

📖 EXPERT READER:

〽 I notice how the author has explained phenomena, and made the connection between science and mystery.

Magnetism was another great mystery to our ancestors. The ancient Greeks noted the mysterious attractive powers of magnetite.

Magnetite is a naturally magnetic mineral that was mined in a region of ancient Greece called Magnesia. The Greeks witnessed that magnetite attracted heavy materials such as iron. They were fascinated by this attraction, but they had no scientific way of understanding what force caused iron to be drawn to magnetite. Instead, they resorted to superstitious explanations, some believing that the magnetite had magical powers or that it possessed a soul.

EXPERT READER:

It's easy to see how ancient people could mistake magnetism for magic, since it's invisible yet produces a visible effect.

It was not until the seventeenth and eighteenth centuries that scientists first began to unravel the mysteries of electricity and magnetism by conducting experiments in controlled environments. They discovered that electric and magnetic phenomena are a result of positive and negative charges interacting with each other.

EXPERT READER:

G The question/answer format is a structure authors frequently use. I can expect the author to begin to answer the question in this section.

G I notice how this subheading connects to the final sentence of the preceding paragraph. The information in this section will most likely build upon and further support that sentence.

℺ The author has used clear language here to begin to explain what electricity is.

What Is Electricity? G
Positive and Negative Charges G

Electricity is a fundamental form of energy. It is the result of charges interacting with each other. ℺ There are two types of charges that are found in all matter. We call these two charges positive and negative. Every material and object in the universe contains both positive and negative charges. The most important thing to remember about positive and negative charges is that like charges repel each other and unlike charges attract each other. Therefore, two positive charges will repel each other, while a positive and a negative charge will attract each other. It is this repulsion and attraction of charges that creates electricity. What we consider electricity is really the motion of charge. G

What Is Magnetism?
The Nature of a Magnet

A magnet is a material or an object that produces a magnetic field. A magnetic field is the force that pulls on other materials, such as iron, and attracts and repels other magnets. We can't actually see a magnetic field, but we can prove that it exists several ways.

A magnet is a dipole. It always has two oppositely charged poles. We call these the north pole of the magnet and the south pole of the magnet. If you bring the like poles of two bar magnets together—north to north or south to south—you will notice that the poles repel, or resist, each other. The opposite is true if you bring unlike poles together. Unlike poles, north to south, attract each other. 📶

The Connection Between Electricity and Magnetism

Now that electricity and magnetism have been discussed, it is time to see how the two are related. Magnetism is in fact nothing more than electric currents. In other words, electricity and magnetism are actually the same thing. 💭

Creating an Electromagnet

A simple experiment will demonstrate that magnetism is simply electric charges in motion. This experiment involves a D cell battery, two lengths of copper wire, an iron nail, a paper clip, and tape. Before the experiment is set up, it will be observed that the nail itself is nonmagnetic. Set the experiment up in the following manner:

- *Strip the plastic casing off each end of the copper wire.*
- *Coil the middle section of the wire neatly around the length of the nail.*
- *Tape the ends of the copper wire to each end of the battery.*

⚜ EXPERT READER:

G The author purposefully included the experiment in this section to support the previous statement that electricity and magnetism are the same thing. After reading this section, I can understand how that is true.

If the experiment is set up correctly, the nail will now attract the paper clip. In other words, the nail will become a magnet. The magnet that is created with the battery, wire, and nail is called an electromagnet.G

Quick Check Self-Evaluation for Analyzing Structure and Evaluating Ideas

Let's take a break here to let the expert reader summarize and evaluate the ideas in this text:

Authors of informational text want to change our thinking in some way or add to our understanding, so the expert reader will think about the most important ideas being discussed in each section of the text and how the text evidence supports that idea(s):

Expert Reader's Summary: Electricity and magnetism have fascinated people throughout history. Although both can seem mysterious, scientific experiments reveal that electricity and magnetism are both the result of positive and negative charges interacting with each other. Two positive charges repel each other, while a positive and a negative charge will attract each other. The attraction and repulsion of charges creates electricity. Experiments prove that magnetism is actually electric currents. Therefore, magnetism and electricity are really the same thing.

Expert Reader: I'm satisfied with this summary. I have thought about the passage carefully, I've reread some sections to check my understanding against text evidence, and I have used key ideas to support the central idea and my summary. I'm ready to challenge my thinking by answering some multiple-choice and written response questions.

Mini Assessment

(Notice that in some cases, more than one answer may be considered correct. It is important to use evidence to build a case for the best answer. Carefully reviewing evidence by returning to the passage will be helpful. Gauging which response is best supported through the evidence is critical.)

1. In the section "Positive and Negative Charges," why does the author include the sentence "Every material and object in the universe contains both positive and negative charges"?

 a) To illustrate the effect electricity can have on every object in the universe.

 b) To identify the connection between positive and negative charges.

 c) To describe how positive and negative charges attract and repel each other.

 d) To explain the motion of change.

2. How does the information in "The Nature of a Magnet" section help to develop the connection between electricity and magnetism?

> a) It argues that we can't actually see a magnetic field.
>
> b) It describes how poles of a magnet attract and repel each other similar to positive and negative charges interacting with each other.
>
> c) It identifies a magnet as a dipole.
>
> d) It explains how electricity and magnetism are related.

3. Reread the last paragraph of the passage. Which sentence most clearly develops the idea that magnetism is electric charge in motion?

> a) Before the experiment is set up, it will be observed that the nail itself is nonmagnetic.
>
> b) Coil the middle section of the wire neatly around the length of the nail.
>
> c) If the experiment is set up correctly, the nail will now attract the paper clip.
>
> d) The magnet that is created with the battery, wire, and the nail is called an electromagnet.

Check your answers. Were you correct?

1. a) is the best answer. We know from this section that electricity is based on positive and negative charges. If every material and object in the universe contains positive and negative charges, electricity has the potential to affect each and every one of these objects.

2. b) is the best answer. We know from earlier sections of the text that electricity occurs when positive and negative charges attract and repel each other. If magnets also attract and repel each other, then they, too, must have positive and negative charges, similar to electricity.

3. c) is the best answer. If the experiment is done correctly, the nail will initially be nonmagnetic until electricity is introduced. Once that is done, the nail becomes magnetic, proving that magnetism is electric charge in motion.

Expert Reader: I'm satisfied with my responses. In all cases, I returned to the text to check against evidence. At times, I had to dig deeply into the text and use clues and inferences while carefully weighing my thinking. I'm confident I can argue in support of my answers with credible evidence from the text. Now I'm ready to try a written response question.

Question: What purpose does the introduction have in this passage? Use evidence from the text to support your answer.

Possible Response: The author uses the introduction to illustrate how superstition and science have been connected in the past when discussing electricity and magnetism. The author explains that natural phenomena, or unusual occurrences that are difficult to explain, like electricity and magnetism, can be explained through scientific processes. When ancient people saw unexplained, mysterious lights in the sky, they had no way to explain them, so they imagined that supernatural forces were controlling the lights. Likewise,

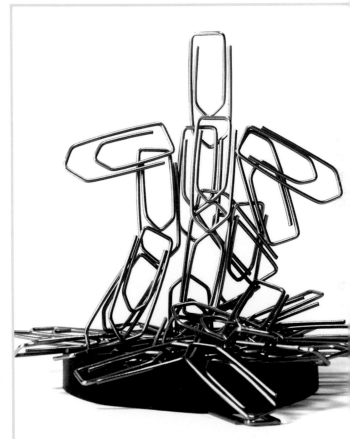

Since a magnetic field is invisible, magnetism was a great mystery to ancient people, who turned to magic to explain its existence.

when the ancient Greeks saw magnetite attract material such as iron, they again resorted to superstitious explanations. When scientific experiments were conducted in the seventeenth and eighteenth centuries, it was discovered that both electricity and magnetism are the result of positive and negative forces interacting with each other. Both are the result of scientific phenomena, not supernatural forces.

Conclusion

How well do you feel you've grasped the expert reader's use of the tips and tricks for analyzing structure and evaluating ideas? Decide if you're ready to move on to the guided practice in the next chapter or if you would like to take another pass through the expert reader's model.

CHAPTER 5

ANALYZING STRUCTURE AND EVALUATING IDEAS IN INFORMATIONAL TEXT: GUIDED PRACTICE

Next, it's time for you to apply the tips and tricks during your close reading of a passage. The practice prompt icons will guide you. Check to see if your responses to the prompts match the provided possible responses.

Chickens and turkeys have always been a favorite food of Americans, partly because they are relatively easy to produce and inexpensive to buy.

Excerpt from:
Poultry, From the Farm to Your Table
by Daniel E. Harmon

Introduction G

Salmonellosis is among the most widely reported food poisons. *Salmonella spp.* is a foodborne bacterium that can cause intestinal infection and other illnesses in people who accidentally eat it. Most victims of salmonellosis poisoning recover within a week, without treatment. For some, abdominal problems are so severe, they need to be hospitalized. For an elderly woman in Sacramento, California, *Salmonella* poisoning in 2011 was fatal. The culprit was believed to be ground turkey distributed by a major meat corporation.

The 2011 salmonellosis tragedy was the latest in a string of food poisonings in contaminated poultry products. In late 2000, the bacterium *Listeria monocytogenes* was detected in turkey products sold in supermarkets and restaurants. Four consumer deaths were blamed on the outbreak.

The possibility of poisoning by salmonellosis or listeriosis is remote. It is a complication, though, in producing one of the nation's favorite foods: poultry. Poultry providers must take great care to avoid poisoning crises.

Almost all the food people buy in supermarkets and restaurants is processed carefully and is safe to eat (although it may be fatty and otherwise unhealthy). Poultry unquestionably has nutritional value. Critics of America's food industry, however, voice concern about how some of the food is produced and processed. At times, flaws in the system result in disaster. G

> ## GUIDED PRACTICE PROMPT:
>
> G How can knowledge of genre help guide your understanding? (Possible response: I believe the author is writing to inform me and make me aware of certain dangers associated with eating poultry. Is he trying to persuade me to not eat poultry as well? I'll need to keep reading to find out.)

Poultry's Rise in Popularity

Beef was the meat of choice in America until 1992. Statistics for that year indicated Americans were eating more chicken than beef. A major reason for the popularity of chicken was the phenomenon of chicken nuggets. But chickens and turkeys have always been among America's favorite foods. Part of the reason is that they are relatively easy to produce and inexpensive to buy. G

> ## GUIDED PRACTICE PROMPT:
>
> G How can I use text structure to build and check understanding? (Possible response: I notice the cause-effect structure of this paragraph.)

What's in That Chicken Nugget You're Eating?

Chicken nuggets were invented in 1983. Because chickens have no "nugget" body parts, you might ask what, exactly, a chicken nugget is. It's a manufactured product. Thirty-eight ingredients have been identified in a popular brand of chicken nugget. Chicken is the primary ingredient, of course. A third of the additional ingredients are corn-based. Nuggets also contain chemicals. Chemicals prevent foaming while the nuggets are being fried, prevent the fat from spoiling, and preserve freshness in the box.

> ## GUIDED PRACTICE PROMPT:
>
> Why did the author include this sidebar? (Possible response: The author is giving me information I may not be aware of. Chicken nuggets don't seem so great anymore. Was this the author's purpose for including the sidebar?)

GUIDED PRACTICE PROMPT:

What are you thinking? (Possible response: Why are the quotation marks around "factories"? I've seem this technique used before when authors are trying to make an important point. Where is poultry raised and processed? Farms or factories?)

Are you being attentive to the author? (Possible response: The author makes unique and surprising comparisons here. Is he trying to persuade me to think a certain way or is he just trying to inform me of circumstances I've been unaware of? Maybe a little of both.)

G How can I use text structure to build and check understanding? (Possible response: This paragraph connects to the introduction and tells me one way poultry can become contaminated—the people who handle the poultry can spread disease.)

What are you thinking? (Possible response: This sounds pretty disgusting. Can these hazards be avoided somehow?)

Poultry "Factories"

Some of the labels and advertisements for poultry items portray sunny, peaceful farm scenes. In reality, most chicken and turkey farms are not pleasant places to visit. The chickens don't wander happily around barnyards and fields. They live their lives packed by the thousand in fenced yards or large barns called grow-out houses. Producers feed them basically the same processed food, and they live the same number of days. Farms are operated largely with machines.

The farms are not as gross, though, as the slaughterhouses. Before it gets to your table, that bird from "Happy Acres" undergoes a series of grim, violent processes. Turkeys and chickens are slaughtered mechanically and carcasses are either cut into pieces (breasts, drumsticks, etc.) or kept whole. Poultry parts are chilled immediately, then packed, frozen, and sent to market. Workers in poultry processing plants must obey careful standards of hygiene because food handlers can spread bacterial diseases that affect the meat products. G

Production and Processing Concerns

Sanitation in poultry houses has been a highly publicized concern. Bird droppings are ever present. Dust and feathers fly. Germs pose hazards to the birds and the humans who work there. Industry watchers worry that packaged meat and eggs can be contaminated if they aren't processed properly.

The problem of foodborne bacteria and other poisons is complicated. Attempts to solve these problems sometimes create problems of their own. For example, in the mid-1990s, a class of antibiotics called quinolones were introduced to cure chickens of certain infections. It was effective, but some strains of the bacteria learned to resist quinolones. These strains presented new threats—to humans. G

Dieticians urge precautions when cooking poultry. Proper cooking is essential to kill *Salmonella spp.* and other poisons. Cooking time is as important as cooking temperature as dietary ailments are not threats if the meat is cooked properly.

Government Regulation

The United States Department of Agriculture (USDA) is the major entity that oversees poultry production. FoodNet is

Many chickens spend their lives in large barns called grow-out houses, where they all eat the same processed food and live the same number of days.

GUIDED PRACTICE PROMPT:

G How can I use text structure to build and check understanding? (Possible response: I'm noticing several cause-effect relationships in this paragraph and the build-up of the problem. Where is the solution?)

What are you thinking? (Possible response: This is important. I finally have a solution to the problem of how humans can avoid becoming ill from contaminated poultry.)

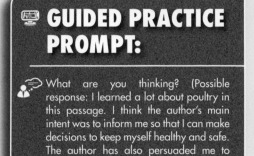

a network of federal and state government agencies that check food samples to make sure they are uncontaminated. Although these regulatory agencies try to ensure safety in the food industry, they are often understaffed and learn of food hazards only after sickness or death has occurred. 💬

Quick Check Self-Evaluation for Analyzing Structure and Evaluating Ideas

At this point, you should be able to summarize this passage. Go ahead and try it! Talk through your answer or jot it down on a separate piece of paper. See the expert reader's analysis for guidance.

Once you're satisfied and have checked your response, challenge your thinking and answer the multiple-choice and written response questions that follow.

Expert Reader's Summary: Poultry is the most popular meat eaten by Americans. As a result, there is a high demand for chicken and turkey. To meet that demand, poultry is frequently raised in a very systematic and mechanical way. Sanitary practices are sometimes difficult to maintain, and there is always the danger of contamination by bacteria. If contaminated chicken is consumed by people, they can become very ill and, in some cases, death can occur. If poultry is properly cooked, the bacteria in any contaminated meat is killed. It is important for people to know this to protect themselves from illness.

Your summary may be somewhat different from the expert reader's, and that's OK, as long as it holds up under scrutiny and squares with the supporting text evidence.

Mini Assessment

(Again, be aware that it is important to use evidence to build a case for the *best* answer. Remember to carefully review evidence by returning to the passage to gauge which response is best supported.)

1. Which sentence in the first paragraph of the passage most *clearly* develops the idea that poultry contamination is a serious and deadly problem?

a) *Salmonella spp.* is a foodborne bacterium that can cause intestinal infection and other illnesses in people who accidentally eat it.

b) Most victims of salmonellosis poisoning recover within a week, without treatment.

c) For an elderly woman in Sacramento, California, *Salmonella* poisoning in 2011 was fatal.

d) The culprit was believed to be ground turkey distributed by a major meat corporation.

2. Closely reread the following sentence from the "What's in That Chicken Nugget You're Eating" sidebar in the passage:

"Because chickens have no 'nugget' body part, you might ask what, exactly, a chicken nugget is."

Why does the author include this sentence in the paragraph?

a) To illustrate how unhealthy chicken nuggets are.

b) To suggest that producers of chicken nuggets are trying to trick people into eating them.

c) To explain the types of chicken parts that are used to make chicken nuggets.

d) To show that chicken nuggets are not food that comes naturally from chickens.

3. How does the information in the first paragraph of the section "Production and Processing Concerns" help to develop the passage?

a) It identifies how *Salmonella spp.* can make its way into our food.

b) It demonstrates how workers process poultry.

c) It describes the way workers keep poultry safe for human consumption.

d) It explains how people can keep themselves safe from *Salmonella spp.*

Check your answers. Were you correct?

1. c) is the best answer. The *Salmonella* poisoning the elderly woman contracted was fatal, or deadly.

2. d) is the best answer. This sentence begins to answer the question posed in the heading of this sidebar—what's in that chicken nugget you're eating? We learn that there are no "nugget" parts of a chicken, which leads us to know that nuggets are not a natural part of a chicken.

3. a) is the best answer. Although the passage starts out with a warning about a deadly bacteria that can affect people when they eat chicken, up until this point, we are not really sure how the bacteria makes its way into poultry. The information in this paragraph identifies how the bacteria makes its way into poultry.

What do you think so far? Is your understanding and analysis of the passage taking shape? Did you return to the passage and find evidence to support your responses? Did your answers square with the

Chicken nuggets are a manufactured product invented in 1983 and have been linked to the growing popularity of chicken in the United States.

evidence? Are you comfortable discussing or writing a response to the following constructed response question? Again, either talk through your answer or jot it down on a separate piece of paper and then check your response against the possible response.

Question: What purpose does the introduction have in this passage? Use evidence from the text to support your answer.

Possible Response: The author uses the introduction to immediately get the reader's attention. The reader quickly understands that contamination of poultry can have deadly consequences for people. We also learn that while most of the poultry we eat is safe, there are occasional flaws in the system used to produce and process poultry. This situation, of course, is of concern because poultry is one of America's favorite and most consumed foods. The introduction "hooks" readers, since we are compelled to continue reading the passage to find out the ways in which we can keep ourselves safe from contaminated poultry.

Conclusion

How well have you grasped the tips and tricks for analyzing structure and evaluating ideas in informational text? Based on your performance and self-evaluation, decide if you've mastered the skills or if you would like to take another pass through this guided practice. Congratulations if you're ready to move on!

A New Expert Reader!

Now that you've mastered how to use the tips and tricks for analyzing structure and evaluating ideas, you're on your way to becoming an expert reader. Continue to practice with different types of literature and informational text. You'll see that your attempts to grapple with classroom and assigned texts are far easier now.

GLOSSARY

ALLEGORY A literary term used to describe a work of literature that includes a deeper-level meaning.

ALLITERATION The repetition of identical or similar initial consonant sounds at the beginning of adjacent or closely connected words.

ANALYZE To carefully examine, inspect, and consider a text in order to fully understand it.

CENTRAL IDEA The key concept or message being expressed.

CLOSE READING The deep, analytical reading of a brief passage of text in which the reader constructs meaning based on author intention and text evidence. The close reading of a text enables readers to gain insights that exceed a cursory reading.

DISTRACTORS Anything that steers a reader away from the text evidence and weakens or misguides analysis.

EVIDENCE Information from the text that a reader uses to prove a position, conclusion, inference, or big idea.

FIX-UP STRATEGIES Common techniques used when meaning is lost.

GENRE A system used to classify types or kinds of writing.

HEADING/SUBHEADING A phrase in larger font or boldface print that provides information on the topic of a section of text.

INFERENCE A conclusion that a reader draws about something by using information that is available.

INFORMATIONAL TEXT A type of nonfiction text, such as articles, essays, opinion piece, or memoirs and historical, scientific, technical, or economic accounts, that is written to give facts or inform about a topic.

LITERATURE Imaginary writing, such as poetry, mysteries, myths, creation stories, science fiction, allegories, and other genres, that tells a story.

PERSUASIVE TEXT A nonfiction text intended to convince the reader of the validity of a set of ideas.

POETIC TECHNIQUE The elements found in poetry, including figurative language, imagery, personification, rhythm, rhyme, repetition, alliteration, assonance, consonance, metaphor, onomatopoeia, and layout of text.

POINT OF VIEW The perspective, or position, from which the story is told.

QUATRAIN A stanza of four lines with a rhyming pattern.

REPETITION Repeating words or phrases to create rhythm and emphasis in poetry.

RHYME The repetition of sound between words or at the end of words, especially at the end of lines.

RHYTHM A strong regular, repeated pattern of sound.

STANZA A group of lines forming the basic unit in a poem.

SUMMARY A short account of a text that gives the main points but not all the details.

TEXT FEATURES The variety of tools used to organize text and to give readers more information about the text.

TEXT STRUCTURE The logical arrangement and organization of ideas in a text using sentences, lines, paragraphs, stanzas, sections, etc.

THEME The central message of a text or what the story is really about.

TONE The writer's communication of an overall feeling or attitude about a book's subject, content, or topic.

Council of Chief State School Officers

One Massachusetts Avenue NW, Suite 700

Washington, DC 20001-1431

(202) 336-7000

Website: http://www.ccsso.org

The Common Core State Standards Initiative is a state-led effort coordinated by the National Governors Association Center for Best Practices (NGA Center) and the Council of Chief State School Officers (CCSSO). The standards provide a clear and consistent framework to prepare students for college and the workforce.

National Association for the Education of Young Children

1313 L Street NW, Suite 500

Washington, DC 20005

(202) 232-8777

Website: http://www.naeyc.org

The National Association for the Education of Young Children is the world's largest organization working on behalf of young children.

National Education Association

1201 16th Street NW

Washington, DC 20036-3290

(202) 833-4000

Website: http://www.nea.org

The National Education Association, the nation's largest professional employee organization, is committed to advancing the cause of public education.

National Parent Teacher Association

12250 North Pitt Street

Alexandria, VA 22314

(703) 518-1200

Website: http://www.pta.org

The National PTA enthusiastically supports the adoption and implementation by all states of the Common Core State Standards. The standards form a solid foundation for high-quality education.

New York State Education Department

89 Washington Avenue

Albany, NY 12234

(518) 474-3852

Website: http://www.engageny.org

EngageNY.org is developed and maintained by the New York State Education Department. This is the official website for current materials and resources related to the implementation of the New York State P–12 Common Core Learning Standards (CCLS).

Partnership for Assessment of Readiness for College and Careers

1400 16th Street NW, Suite 510

Washington, DC 20036

(202)745-2311

Website: http://www.parcconline.org

The Partnership for Assessment of Readiness for College and Careers (PARCC) is a consortium of eighteen states, plus the District of Columbia and the U.S. Virgin Islands, working together to develop a common set of K–12 assessments in English and math anchored in what it takes to be ready for college and careers.

U.S. Department of Education

Department of Education Building

400 Maryland Avenue SW
Washington, DC 20202
(800) 872-5327
Website: http://www.edu.gov
Nearly every state has adopted the Common Core State Standards. The
federal government has supported this state-led effort by helping ensure
that higher standards are being implemented for all students and that
educators are being supported in transitioning to new standards.

Websites

Due to the changing nature of Internet links, Rosen Publishing has developed
an online list of websites related to the subject of this book. This site is updated
regularly. Please use this link to access the list:

http://www.rosenlinks.com/CCRGR/Struct

BIBLIOGRAPHY

Beers, Kylene, and Robert E. Probst. *Notice & Note: Strategies for Close Reading*. Portsmouth, NH: Heinemann, 2013

Frost, Robert. *The Exposed Nest*, Mountain Interval Collection, Henry Holt and Company, 1916. (Public Domain)

Frost, Robert. *The Pasture,* North of Boston Collection, Henry Holt and Company, 1915. (Public Domain)

Galiano, Dean. *Science Made Simple: Electric and Magnetic Phenomena*. New York, NY: Rosen Publishing, 2011.

Harmon, Daniel E. *Poultry: From the Farm to Your Table*. New York, NY: Rosen Publishing, 2012.

Pinnell, Gay Su, and Irene C. Fountas. *Genre Study: Teaching with Fiction and Nonfiction Books*. Portsmouth, NH: Heinemann, 2012

Poe, Edgar Allan. "The Bells." 1849. (Public Domain)

Poe, Edgar Allan. *Eldorado*. 1849. (Public Domain)

About the Authors

Sandra K. Athans is a National Board Certified practicing classroom teacher with fifteen years of experience teaching reading and writing at the elementary level. She is the author of several teacher-practitioner books on literacy, including *Quality Comprehension* and *Fun-tastic Activities for Differentiating Comprehension Instruction*, both published by the International Reading Association. Athans has presented her research at the International Reading Association, the National Council of Teachers of English Conferences, and the New York State Reading Association Conferences. Her contributions have appeared in well-known literacy works including *The Literacy Leadership Handbook* and *Strategic Writing Mini-Lessons*. She is also a children's book writer and specializes in high-interest, photo-informational books published with Millbrook Press.

Athans earned a B.A. in English from the University of Michigan, an M.A. in elementary education from Manhattanville College, and an M.S. in literacy from Le Moyne College. She is also certified to teach secondary English. In addition to teaching in the classroom, she is an adjunct professor at Le Moyne College and provides instruction in graduate-level literacy classes. This spring she was named an outstanding elementary social studies educator by the Central New York Council for the Social Studies. She serves on various ELA leadership networks and collaborates with educators nationwide to address the challenges of the Common Core Standards. The Tips and Tricks series is among several Common Core resources she has authored for Rosen Publishing.

Robin W. Parente is a practicing reading specialist and classroom teacher with more than fifteen years of experience teaching reading and writing at the elementary level. She also serves as the elementary

ELA coordinator for a medium-sized district in central New York, working with classroom teachers to implement best literacy practices in the classroom. Parente earned a B.S. in elementary education and an M.S. in education/literacy from the State University of New York at Oswego. She is a certified reading specialist (PK–12) and elementary classroom teacher and has served on various ELA leadership networks to collaborate with educators to address the challenges of the Common Core Standards. The Tips and Tricks series is among several Common Core resources she has authored for Rosen Publishing.

Photo Credits

Designer: Nicole Russo; Editor: Bethany Bryan;
Photo Researcher: Cindy Reiman